MW01296095

Effective
Financial Management
for Non-Profits

By: Donald F. Clarke

Effective Financial Management for Non-Profits

Copyright 2014 by Don Clarke Enterprises, Inc.

All Rights Reserved. No part of this book may be transmitted or reproduced in any form by any means without advanced written permission from the publisher.

Designer: Corain Cash

Editors: Jose Santodomingo, CPA

FIRST EDITION

Printed and bound in the United States of America

First Printing, May 2014

ISBN-13: 978-0-9916093-0-7

Library of Congress Control Number: 2014904280

Dedication

. . . .

This book is dedicated to my life partner, friend, advocate and counselor, Dr. Helga A. Clarke. Her stewardship of my family and its finances, done with remarkable excellence, has allowed me the latitude to pursue the things that I have been able to do over our 37 years of marriage. Thanks first lady, you are the wind beneath my wings!

I also dedicate this book to my four (4) wonderful children, Don Jr., Keturah, Simone and Dwight and my grandchildren, who have made me the happiest man on Earth.

Contents

Introduction

Effectively managing finances in the Twenty First Century economy is the quintessential challenge for churches and non-profits. With charitable giving down across the map, the Pastor or President of the charitable giving organization must also know how to properly manage finances in order to maintain proper liquidity. We are called upon to understand current financial metrics trending in our organizations; comparing them to historical data and industry comparisons so we can manage inflows and outflows.

The Pastor/President must have a basic understanding of cash flow, liquidity, budgeting and interpretation of financial metrics in order to be able to talk intelligently and offer guidance to those they lead. A basic knowledge of how financial statements are prepared and the narrative they convey is essential in my opinion for the Pastor/President. The reasoning is that while someone else might be responsible for incurring, extrapolating and submitting the data to the Pastor/President, he or she is ultimately responsible for understanding these numbers. The "buck" stops with the head of the organization and in most organizations the Pastor/President is the Chief Executive Officer ("CEO") and the highest level of accountability within the organization. In my opinion, ignorance is not "bliss" and cannot be used as an excuse.

"Too many times the Pastor/President is busy trying to get folks to heaven while the organization's finances are on their way to hell." ("Clarkeism")

My friends, churches and non-profits are businesses, therefore proper financial management is a key ingredient to their reputations, successes and longevity.

Thanks for taking this journey with me. In this book I will attempt to have a one-on-one "dinner table conversation" with you, where I will try to avoid big words and complex financial jargon and just merely focus on how much you take in, how much you expend and how to know, watch and manage these 2 streams, one of inflows and the other of outflows.

As you follow along with me you will see that from time to time I will use certain "Clarkeisms". If you are now wondering what a "Clarkeism" is, it is simply a phrase that I have coined over my 62 years of living of key things that I should remember. So here is another "Clarkeism" that will be a theme throughout this book: *"Never spend more than you take in and never spend everything that you take in"*. I can figuratively hear your minds going off but be patient, I will clarify this as we take this journey together!

Having been a Pastor since I was 28 years old and also having worked and even now still working in the banking sector, I have amassed a wealth of knowledge over these 34 years that I am anxious to share with you, especially if you are just starting out. Oh how I wish I had a mentor that would have helped me avoid some of the pitfalls that I fell into, some all for the better! While experience is a great teacher, it can be awfully expensive so hopefully I can help you reduce some of these often avoidable expenses!

Thanks for buying this book and I hope you find it refreshing, enlightening and informational. Remember that *"information without transformation leads to frustration."* ("Clarkeism")

May my God prosper you in all that you do, especially in your finances!

Chapter One
The Bible and Money Management

Chapter One
The Bible and Money Management

The world's wisest man, Solomon, was blessed by God extraordinarily with this trait called wisdom because he specifically sought after it and he had some choice nuggets on debt and money management which he has left behind for us all to ponder. In Proverbs 22:26-27, he cautions us about acquiring debt before we have determined that we can repay such a debt. To venture into debt obligations before ensuring that one has the means to repay such debt is irresponsible, precipitous and is like a hunter who shoots first and aims after.

> "Do not be one who shakes hands in pledge or puts up security for debts; if you lack the means to pay, your very bed will be snatched from under you."
>
> **Proverbs 22:26-27**

In the year 2013, I have looked at the financial statements of many churches who continue to borrow heavily to finance operations when they have no plausible means of repaying such debt. Danger lurks here as Solomon eluded, and we have seen more churches closing at a rate of 7,000 per year and many falling into foreclosure. Not only are these organizations losing the very bed the Pastor sleeps on as Solomon eludes, but the pulpit from where to preach the Gospel; the main purpose for which churches exist.

I am often conflicted, as are some of my peers, about how much time and energy should be spent on debt and money management and whether or not we should outsource such a function. Firstly, I believe that the non-profit is a business and has to be run like one. As such, we need to understand how regular businesses operate and how they manage money.

Let us look at firstly capitalizing a business. Most business owners capitalize their businesses with equity injections or putting "skin in the game". Such capital represents "seed money" or equity to help establish and finance business growth. Next to help them grow even more and expand, businesses often borrow funds for working capital support or to acquire property, plant and equipment that they need to drive business revenue.

One can argue then that most businesses use a combination of debt and equity to start and grow businesses. This has to be carefully thought out because while equity is interest free, debt comes with payback requirements and interest charges.

Okay, you are now saying "transition this to the non-profit"! The non-profit has no owners to inject equity. The seed capital comes from membership tax deductible contributions. The non-profit must also secure "seed money" from its members to start up but also equally important, like regular businesses who retain a part of their earnings to boost their equity and ease their debt reliance, the non-profit must always seek to retain a part of its intake. Remember this "Clarkeism", *"Never spend more than you take in and never spend everything you take in".*

In terms of debt, how much should a non-profit borrow, if it borrows at all? Deuteronomy 28:12 I am afraid, creates quite a dilemma and conundrum for us.

> "The Lord will open the heavens, the storehouse of his bounty, to send rain on your land in season and to bless all the work of your hands. You will lend to many nations but will borrow from none."
>
> **Deuteronomy 28:12**

God, speaking through Moses, was challenging Israel to put Him to the test. He explicitly promised that if they obeyed Him, He would bless them greatly and that they would "…lend to many nations and not borrow". What does this mean? I believe God at His word and so if His people, especially His non-profits, could live without debt that would be ideal. However, in today's fast-paced society where huge buildings, huge congregations and giant networks are benchmarks for "successful" ministries, borrowing has become an integral part of ministry forever. So then we must deal with the situations as they exist in the 21st century! I know I will be reminded that when David and Solomon collaborated on the building of the Temple, it was totally donation and not debt driven. I believe the Bible and God already made provisions for Deuteronomy 28:12, just like He has throughout the Bible when His people (myself included) have strayed from His initial intent.

That is why in later books of the Bible, we then see it mentioning debt and repayment as in the earlier quote from Proverbs 22:26-27 and the following:

> "Do not be one who shakes hands in pledge or puts up security for debts; if you lack the means to pay, your very bed will be snatched from under you."
>
> **Proverbs 22:26-27**

> "The wicked borrows and does not repay, but the righteous gives generously"
>
> **Psalms 37:21**

Firstly, we are reminded that debt acquisition must be married to a debt repayment plan. Secondly, we are categorized with the wicked if we fail to repay legitimate debt that we willingly and knowingly entered into. This might get me into some hot water but repayment of the non-profit's debt should be a priority and planned for, ahead of all other expenditures.

Listen to Elijah's instructions to the widow whose husband had died and left her with insurmountable debt:

> "She went and told the man of God, and he said, Go, sell the oil and pay your debts. You and your sons can live on what is left."
>
> **2 Kings 4:7**

She was told to repay her debts firstly and then live off the remainder and not the other way around. What do you think?

Debt Management

> "Whoever can be trusted with very little can also be trusted with much, and whoever is dishonest with very little will also be dishonest with much."
>
> **Luke 16:10**

This passage articulated by the Master Himself seems to suggest that in terms of Kingdom resources, He likes us to start off with small amounts so that He can evaluate our stewardship skills. This runs counter today to what I observe in ministry. No one it seems wants to start small and hone their skills before becoming a large "mega" ministry. Stewardship skills and the learning of them take time and sometimes come by trial and error.

We need to experience the "training wheel" stage and master that before we are given the keys to the Ferrari. Starting small allows us to build the infrastructure or foundation on which to expand responsibly. Proper financial management is at the core of every successful non-profit.

> "Go to the ant, you sluggard; consider its ways and be wise! It has no commander, no overseer or ruler, yet it stores its provisions in summer and gathers its food at harvest."
>
> **Proverbs 6:6-8**

This passage written by Solomon the wise man seems to suggest that proper resource management and planning is instinctive because the ant does not have a brain but uses instinct to manage its resources well. So then, humans with brains should at least be as wise as the ant!

In noting the two disciplines the ant deploys we learn that it:

a) **Stores its provisions in summer**. This means that it does not eat everything it gathers! Remember the "Clarkeism", *"Never spend everything you take in"*? Experience has taught me in particular that ministry finances can be sporadic, cyclical, seasonal and all of the above. Just like the ant gathers in the summer and thinks ahead for the winter, ministries must develop the same mindset!

b) **Gathers its food at harvest**. Not every day is harvest and most harvests are seasonal. I was once told that in its heyday, a ministry took in so much money they did not know what to do with it. But then something happened and the finances fell off by double digit percentages. How a ministry does in harvest prepares it for leaner times. The story of Joseph in Egypt is a good example of stewardship and planning ahead for leaner times. *"Never spend everything you take in!"*

Chapter Two
How Much Should Your Budget Be?

Chapter Two
How Much Should Your Budget Be?

What does the Bible have to say about budgets and money management? Plenty! Both the Old and New Testaments are filled with references about money and its management. According to my esteemed and learned friend Dr. Patrick Pang, PhD (The Seed Company, Los Angeles, California), there are 2,450 references in the Bible regarding finances and money management.

> "Suppose one of you wants to build a tower. Won't you first sit down and estimate the cost to see if you have enough money to complete it? For if you lay the foundation and are not able to finish it, everyone who sees it will ridicule you, saying, 'this person began to build and wasn't able to finish'."
>
> **Luke 14:28-30**

Jesus in one of His many teachable moments with His disciples introduced the process of building and budget construction. Who can argue that He was speaking about the cost of discipleship? It is difficult to ignore the analogy of the tower builder and his need for a budget to avoid embarrassment.

This is not a nuanced argument. It is plain and simple; plans to build and a budget should precede the actual start of the building. The budgeting process helps us understand what resources we have available to us compared to the cost of the operation. A budget should precede a proposed project in addition to year-to-year projections for existing facilities. The methodology of preparing one will be discussed in later chapters.

Listen to Solomon, the author of Proverbs and the wisest man who ever lived and managed a vast and wealthy empire. Notice he uses key words such as wisdom, understanding and knowledge, which are precursors to a building whose rooms are filled with "rare and beautiful treasures". Success in finances does not occur by happenstance, it is planned and deliberate.

> "By wisdom a house is built, and through understanding it is established; through knowledge its rooms are filled with rare and beautiful treasures."
>
> **Proverbs 24:3-4**

I am often asked, by Pastors of existing churches and start-ups alike, how much a budget should be. So I think it is important to address this answer geared towards two distinct and separate audiences, namely the established church and the start up.

The Established Church Budget

For the established church, the route to developing a budget is a much easier one than for the start up. The established church has historical metrics both in terms of membership, attendance, and inflow and outflow numbers on which to properly construct a "realistic" budget.

To begin, the budgetary process should look back at say the last 3 years to see what the attendance, membership and giving metrics have been. Then, using percentile trajectories, the budget can be created to provide the most predictable results. Please do not take me down the "faith" trip here! Of course we are people of faith and yes we serve a Super-natural God who knows no challenges and with whom all things are possible. Yes, but He also wants us to be realistic in our budgetary processes and not have a budgeted income of $10 million, for example, when over the last 3 years you have averaged $100,000. As my grandson Shane would say, "Really?"!

What I suggest that you do is look at the income trending over the last three (3) years and let's say for example that giving has been increasing year-over-year at a 7% clip. Then the upcoming budget should reflect the average of the last 3 years. I normally like to "flatten" this out for the most conservative approach so that for example, if giving metric increases have been say 5%, 7% and 9% over the prior 3 years, then I would use 7% on my projections for the upcoming year which is calculated as $5+7+9=21/3=7\%$. This conservative approach ignores the 2 outlier years, the one at 5% and the other at 9%, and produces a number in the middle. If I exceed that number, bravo! But one should not only use the latest year, which is the highest of the three, just in case that was an aberration.

By the way as you will observe later in this book, I prefer that budgets be done on a month-over-month ("MOM") basis, and then rolled up into the annual numbers. Also when looking back over the year-over-year ("YOY") comparisons also look at the MOM trending and also period-over-period ("POP") trending. These 3 acronyms I came up with over my 25+ years of teaching Financial Analysis for the Commercial Finance Association ("CFA"), is an easy way for my audience to remember the necessary comparisons in financial analysis and budget construction. This approach (once you get a grasp of all these acronyms) allows you to understand cyclical and seasonal aberrations in financial information trending and how to predict how much comes in and when.

I also suggest that for any new projects to be undertaken, either a separate budget is prepared or line items highlighting related income and expenses unique to this project be separated out.

Also, please scrutinize the inflows and look for unusual gifts that will spike your revenue but might not be repeated the following year. Please let us not go down this "faith" trip again!

In the same way, expenses that are a "one-of" should be again excluded to properly reflect what the predictable expenses should be. One last thing for income projections: always do one where the intake remains the same as the year before and see if they can bear any added expenditures without plunging the organization into red ink. This is what I refer to as a "stress test" to see how much expenses can be absorbed at prevailing revenue rates before the ministry implodes. As common sense would normally tell, it is easier to increase expenses than revenue.

The Start-Up Church Budget

The budget for the start-up church is filled with challenges and has to be well thought out. If you are an independent with no denominational support, then you must sit down and:

1) Realistically count the heads of who will be entering this endeavor with you.
2) Decide how much income you can reasonably expect from them to help the ministry until others start attending.
3) Seek verbal or written commitments for at least 1 year from them.

Only once you have locked up your commitments should you start seeking a place to rent because you can get locked into a lease that if you cannot pay, could become legally and financially problematic. Here are some other start-up tidbits one might find helpful:

1. Do not be afraid to start small. I started in my living room for example until I built up some cash reserves. This is not always the best solution because you are then bringing folks into your home. This, if it happens to be the route, should have a limited shelf life and not go on for too long.

2. One caution to the start-up, save as much as you can! Keep your expenses realistic. *"Never spend more than you take in and never spend everything you take in!"* ("Clarkeism")

3. Plan on taking no salaries or adding full time staff until you can afford it. As for the big cars and airplanes…really? Remember that you are just starting up.

Why save? Because you should strive to, as soon as financially possible, to acquire your own building. Remember the tenant is a slave to the landlord and if you're going to struggle to pay his rent, you might as well do so to pay your own mortgage. *"God is an owner, not a renter!"* ("Clarkeism")

In terms of projecting membership growth metrics, which eventually results in growth in revenues, a demographical study should be done on the area where the ministry is located. This study should bear in mind the average travel time of the area surveyed to the ministry location, which should be within a 30 minute window. The study should include:

- Number of residents
- Average household income
- Number of churches within the area

While this list is not all-inclusive, this should provide a good basis for projecting attendance and giving. Please also bear in mind that:

1) Attendance is always the leading indicator to giving and
2) The latter is a trailing indicator.

What that means is that it takes some time for giving to catch up with attendance.

The following represents an annual sample budget that lists all the revenue and expenses for an established ministry.

Sample Budget – XYZ Church

XYZ Church	Budget
Cash Sources:	2013
Tithes & Offering	$ 12,631,950.54
Health & Fitness	280,000.00
Church Campaign	150,000.00
Mail-In	265,000.00
Ministry Offerings	113,500.00
Ministry Deposits	164,100.00
Rental Income	169,464.00
Bookstore Sales	262,100.00
Plus: Anticipated Cash Receipts	**$ 14,036,114.54**
Cash Uses:	
Lender Debt Service	$ 3,433,000.00
Bank Debt Service	51,242.49
Church Payroll	4,913,096.63
Insurance (Health)	585,000.00
Insurance (P/C)	328,944.24
In-House Contractors	788,820.00
Lease Payments	589,020.00
Duplication Product	45,000.00
Missionary Support	78,433.33
Trash	24,000.00
Water	156,000.00
Natural Gas	42,808.80
Power	1,037,380.96
Telephone	276,000.00
Bookstore product	102,025.00
Pastoral Care	80,613.00
Outreach	12,600.00
Guest Speaker	55,000.00
Legal and Professional	306,000.00
Operations	711,000.00
Credit card	180,000.00
Minus: Anticipated Cash Payments	**$ 13,795,984.45**
Excess Cash Receipts over Cash Payments	**$ 240,130.09**

The summation from the foregoing figures is that the ministry is projecting that it will generate a net cash of $240K after meeting all its expenses, including paying its mortgage payments to the lender.

It is important to remember that a "MOM" presentation be done especially as far as revenue is concerned. Most ministries experience cyclical giving whereby the summer months are usually slow and following there is a 4th quarter surge. Despite the cyclicality of the revenue however, most expenses are fixed and evenly spaced out. That means that one month the ministry could have a surplus but a deficit the next month.

XYZ Church, Inc.
Sample Budget

	Budget Total Revenue
Anticipated Cash Receipts	$ 14,036,114.54
Cash Uses:	
Lender Debt Service Debt Service	$ 3,433,000.00
Ban k Debt Service	51,242.49
Church Payroll	4,913,096.63
Insurance (Health)	585,000.00
Insurance (P/C)	328,944.24
In-House Contractors	788,820.00
Lease Payments	589,020.00
Duplication Product	45,000.00
Missionary Support	78,433.33
Trash	24,000.00
Water	156,000.00
Natural Gas	42,808.80
Power	1,037,380.96
Telephone	276,000.00
Bookstore product	102,025.00
Pastoral Care	80,613.00
Outreach	12,600.00
Guest Speaker	55,000.00
Legal and Professional	306,000.00
Operations	711,000.00
Credit card	180,000.00
Minus: Anticipated Cash Payments	$ 13,795,984.45
Excess Cash Receipts over Cash Payments	$ 240,130.09

1st Quarter Review

		January	February	March
Anticipated Cash Receipts		1,368,521.16	1,169,676.21	1,169,676.21
Cash Uses:				
Lender Debt Service Debt Service	$	286,083.33 $	286,083.33 $	286,083.33
Ban k Debt Service		4,270.21	4,270.21	4,270.21
Church Payroll		409,424.72	409,424.72	409,424.72
Insurance (Health)		48,750.00	48,750.00	48,750.00
Insurance (P/C)		27,412.02	27,412.02	27,412.02
In-House Contractors		65,735.00	65,735.00	65,735.00
Lease Payments		49,085.00	49,085.00	49,085.00
Duplication Product		3,750.00	3,750.00	3,750.00
Missionary Support		6,536.11	6,536.11	6,536.11
Trash		2,000.00	2,000.00	2,000.00
Water		13,000.00	13,000.00	13,000.00
Natural Gas		3,567.40	3,567.40	3,567.40
Power		86,448.41	86,448.41	86,448.41
Telephone		23,000.00	23,000.00	23,000.00
Bookstore product		8,502.08	8,502.08	8,502.08
Pastoral Care		6,717.75	6,717.75	6,717.75
Outreach		1,050.00	1,050.00	1,050.00
Guest Speaker		4,583.33	4,583.33	4,583.33
Legal and Professional		25,500.00	25,500.00	25,500.00
Operations		59,250.00	59,250.00	59,250.00
Credit card		15,000.00	15,000.00	15,000.00
Minus: Anticipated Cash Payments	$	1,149,665.37 $	1,149,665.37 $	1,149,665.37
Excess Cash Receipts over Cash Payments	$	**218,855.79** $	**20,010.84** $	**20,010.84**

Actual Receipts
Actual Expenses
Variance

Please note in the first quarter that January shows a surge in revenue, thus driving a larger bottom line retention. This is because there is an anticipated surge in revenue for New Year's Sunday, which is usually a highly attended service. In the ensuing months February and March, revenue returns to normalcy.

2nd Quarter Review

	April	May	June
Anticipated Cash Receipts	1,169,676.21	1,169,676.21	1,169,676.21
Cash Uses:			
Lender Debt Service Debt Service	$ 286,083.33	$ 286,083.33	$ 286,083.33
Ban k Debt Service	4,270.21	4,270.21	4,270.21
Church Payroll	409,424.72	409,424.72	409,424.72
Insurance (Health)	48,750.00	48,750.00	48,750.00
Insurance (P/C)	27,412.02	27,412.02	27,412.02
In-House Contractors	65,735.00	65,735.00	65,735.00
Lease Payments	49,085.00	49,085.00	49,085.00
Duplication Product	3,750.00	3,750.00	3,750.00
Missionary Support	6,536.11	6,536.11	6,536.11
Trash	2,000.00	2,000.00	2,000.00
Water	13,000.00	13,000.00	13,000.00
Natural Gas	3,567.40	3,567.40	3,567.40
Power	86,448.41	86,448.41	86,448.41
Telephone	23,000.00	23,000.00	23,000.00
Bookstore product	8,502.08	8,502.08	8,502.08
Pastoral Care	6,717.75	6,717.75	6,717.75
Outreach	1,050.00	1,050.00	1,050.00
Guest Speaker	4,583.33	4,583.33	4,583.33
Legal and Professional	25,500.00	25,500.00	25,500.00
Operations	59,250.00	59,250.00	59,250.00
Credit card	15,000.00	15,000.00	15,000.00
Minus: Anticipated Cash Payments	$ 1,149,665.37	$ 1,149,665.37	$ 1,149,665.37
Excess Cash Receipts over Cash Payments	$ 20,010.84	$ 20,010.84	$ 20,010.84

Actual Receipts
Actual Expenses
Variance

The revenue for the second quarter is shown as static, although Easter falls within this quarter and might cause a spike in revenue in March or April.

3rd Quarter Review

		July		August		September
Anticipated Cash Receipts		**1,052,708.61**		**994,224.81**		**1,029,315.06**
Cash Uses:						
Lender Debt Service Debt Service	$	286,083.33	$	286,083.33	$	286,083.33
Ban k Debt Service		4,270.21		4,270.21		4,270.21
Church Payroll		409,424.72		409,424.72		409,424.72
Insurance (Health)		48,750.00		48,750.00		48,750.00
Insurance (P/C)		27,412.02		27,412.02		27,412.02
In-House Contractors		65,735.00		65,735.00		65,735.00
Lease Payments		49,085.00		49,085.00		49,085.00
Duplication Product		3,750.00		3,750.00		3,750.00
Missionary Support		6,536.11		6,536.11		6,536.11
Trash		2,000.00		2,000.00		2,000.00
Water		13,000.00		13,000.00		13,000.00
Natural Gas		3,567.40		3,567.40		3,567.40
Power		86,448.41		86,448.41		86,448.41
Telephone		23,000.00		23,000.00		23,000.00
Bookstore product		8,502.08		8,502.08		8,502.08
Pastoral Care		6,717.75		6,717.75		6,717.75
Outreach		1,050.00		1,050.00		1,050.00
Guest Speaker		4,583.33		4,583.33		4,583.33
Legal and Professional		25,500.00		25,500.00		25,500.00
Operations		59,250.00		59,250.00		59,250.00
Credit card		15,000.00		15,000.00		15,000.00
Minus: Anticipated Cash Payments	$	1,149,665.37	$	1,149,665.37	$	1,149,665.37
Excess Cash Receipts over Cash Payments	$	**(96,956.76)**	$	**(155,440.56)**	$	**(120,350.31)**
Actual Receipts						
Actual Expenses						
Variance						

The summer months are when revenue show their steepest decline. Folks take off on vacation and somehow seem to forget that ministry requires year round support.

By the way, today's ministry must engage its members/givers to use the internet, utilizing tools such as Paypal; an emerging venue through which to give. Some ministries like ours are experiencing that up to 20% of weekly intake comes through internet giving. Please note that in the summer months of July, August and September, the ministry experiences cash losses but such losses are more than made up for in the comeback months of January and December. Careful planning will ensure that some of the excess garnered in December and January are set aside for the leaner summer months.

"Go to the ant, you sluggard; consider its ways and be wise! It has no commander, no overseer or ruler, yet it stores its provisions in summer and gathers its food at harvest."
Proverbs 6:6-8

4th Quarter Review

	October	November	December
Anticipated Cash Receipts	1,169,676.21	1,169,676.21	1,403,611.41
Cash Uses:			
Lender Debt Service Debt Service	$ 286,083.33	$ 286,083.33	$ 286,083.33
Ban k Debt Service	$ 4,270.21	$ 4,270.21	$ 4,270.21
Church Payroll	$ 409,424.72	$ 409,424.72	$ 409,424.72
Insurance (Health)	$ 48,750.00	$ 48,750.00	$ 48,750.00
Insurance (P/C)	$ 27,412.02	$ 27,412.02	$ 27,412.02
In-House Contractors	$ 65,735.00	$ 65,735.00	$ 65,735.00
Lease Payments	$ 49,085.00	$ 49,085.00	$ 49,085.00
Duplication Product	$ 3,750.00	$ 3,750.00	$ 3,750.00
Missionary Support	$ 6,536.11	$ 6,536.11	$ 6,536.11
Trash	$ 2,000.00	$ 2,000.00	$ 2,000.00
Water	$ 13,000.00	$ 13,000.00	$ 13,000.00
Natural Gas	$ 3,567.40	$ 3,567.40	$ 3,567.40
Power	$ 86,448.41	$ 86,448.41	$ 86,448.41
Telephone	$ 23,000.00	$ 23,000.00	$ 23,000.00
Bookstore product	$ 8,502.08	$ 8,502.08	$ 8,502.08
Pastoral Care	$ 6,717.75	$ 6,717.75	$ 6,717.75
Outreach	$ 1,050.00	$ 1,050.00	$ 1,050.00
Guest Speaker	$ 4,583.33	$ 4,583.33	$ 4,583.33
Legal and Professional	$ 25,500.00	$ 25,500.00	$ 25,500.00
Operations	$ 59,250.00	$ 59,250.00	$ 59,250.00
Credit card	$ 15,000.00	$ 15,000.00	$ 15,000.00
Minus: Anticipated Cash Payments	$ 1,149,665.37	$ 1,149,665.37	$ 1,149,665.37
Excess Cash Receipts over Cash Payments	**$ 20,010.84**	**$ 20,010.84**	**$ 253,946.04**

Actual Receipts
Actual Expenses
Variance

The fourth quarter numbers are flattening out in October and November and then spike to an annual high driven by the Christmas and Watch Night giving, which add two new revenue days to the mix.

Budgetary Nuggets

1. Remember the old adage, what comes first, the chicken or the egg? How do I handle this financial dilemma?! Where do I start?

   ❖ Start with a budget – This is not as complex as the chicken and the egg dilemma.

2. Do not reinvent the wheel. Others have gone before you and you did not invent ministry!

   ❖ Get historical information and learn from the successes and failures of your predecessors.

3. Remember that nothing in ministry is usually free, not even advice!

   ❖ Employ a qualified financial CFO and surround that person with an external CPA and maybe even a Financial Consultant, a team of which can offer sound budgetary advice and construction.

4. Ministry should be treated like a business venture!

   ❖ Would you want to invest your life savings in an organization without the foresight of constructing a budget?

5. Understanding the difference between fixed and variable expenses is crucial for the Pastor/President to know.

   ❖ Pay attention to the fixed expenses and manage the variables well! Resist the urge to go on a compulsive shopping spree that will render the budget useless and plunge the organization into financial chaos. Stick to the script.

Something to answer as you wrap up your budget construction and roll out these numbers to those you lead: How does your budget reflect your priorities?

Can I be honest here? My struggle has been and still is how to reconcile the need for what I call ministry essentials, such as feeding the poor and having maximum social impact, with the realities of my organization's financial position.

Many Pastors are visionaries who cast a wide vision as to what their ministry should look like but they also need to come to grasp with the realities on the ground. Easier said than done!

Chapter Three
Evaluating Financial Performance

Chapter Three
Evaluating Financial Performance

Effectively managing finances begins with proper accounting policies and procedures. Internal controls and disciplines are at the core of good financial management. Too many times I have seen the church ran like a candy store or the Pastor's personal business. When it is done that way, it has concocted a recipe destined for disaster and will eventually attract regulatory and IRS scrutiny.

The following are what I think demonstrates good internal controls and disciplines for the non-profit:

❖ The financial maintenance and reporting should be under the supervision of an internal Chief Financial Officer ("CFO") who, while reporting to the Pastor/President, should preferably not be the Pastor nor any close relative. This gives the resemblance of "arm's length" control and adds an air of autonomy and integrity to this crucial function.

❖ There should be adequate checks and balances in the intake and disbursement of funds. For example, at least two (2) people should collaborate on funds intake so there is accountability and transparency. Secondly, there should be at least two (2) signatures required on checks over a certain "pre-set" amount. One of the signors can be the Pastor/President/CEO but the counter-signor should be an independent third party.

❖ There should be regular interim financial reporting whether it is monthly or quarterly but at least quarterly. This allows the senior management to be aware of the current financial trending metrics of the organization so that it can make adjustments if necessary in "real-time". It is inexcusable to only have year-end financial statements.

Listen to Proverbs 27:23:

> "Be sure you know the condition of your flocks; give careful attention to your herds"
> **Proverbs 27:23**

It is important to know what the current financial condition of the organization is and on a real-time basis. The shepherd cannot wait until year-end to take stock of his herd. If the flock was missing members, waiting a year to find that out would be almost criminally negligent.

❖ There should be a proper accounting system in place that is designed uniquely for non-profits and while I will not endorse one specifically, I can tell you that there are a myriad of these systems available. A good system will provide not only summary financials but detailed giving profiles and demographics of revenue base. While internal interim financials are okay, I believe that the ministry should engage the services of a qualified Certified Public Accountant ("CPA") to handle its year end reporting. As a matter of fact, most institutional lenders require such reporting on an annual basis as a part of their loan and security agreements and consider it an event of default if one is not provided.

Having now gone through what I believe are the elements of good infrastructure in the financial accounting of the non-profit, let's now tackle interpreting and analyzing the data produced by such systems.

Financial analysis at its core includes both vertical and horizontal analyses of financial statements. Vertical means looking down from north to south on the balance sheet and the income statements while horizontal entails comparing the current data to historic performances. The balance sheet is merely a listing of what the organization owns, how much it owes and what the equity is or the difference between owned and owed. The income statement summarizes the intakes and outflows of the organization with the "change in net assets" being the difference of the two.

For effectiveness, the comparisons must be made contextually, meaning that periodic comparison must utilize the POP theory (remember that?), while year ends utilize the YOY principle. Where does MOM fit in? Usually MOM is applied when comparing projections to actual data to see how close one comes to the other.

Understanding the Balance Sheet

Before we can begin to analyze the balance sheet, we must understand what the balance sheet is and how it functions. The balance sheet is made up of three (3) segments: Assets, Liabilities and Equity.

➤ **Assets** are those things that the ministry owns which range from cash in the bank to property (real estate) and equipment.

➤ **Liabilities** are comprised of how much the ministry owes and to whom.

➤ **Equity** is simply the difference between the assets (which should be greater) and the liabilities.

When liabilities (what is owed) is greater than what is owned, the organization is technically insolvent/bankrupt as it does not have ample assets to liquidate and pay its liabilities.

It is important to note that the greater the "equity" or "skin in the game", the lesser the reliance on outside sources to finance the organization's operations.

I feel compelled to remind us all that debt is never "free" and that is why it is referred to as "debt burden" in some circles. Debt minimization leads to more retention of revenue down to equity eventually because the cost of debt is lessened. One calculation or metric that I always look at is what is called the Debt-to-Worth ("DTW") ratio. It is not only key in "for profit" entities but also non-profit entities. This metric is calculated by dividing the total debt by the entity's equity. This is commonly referred to as "leverage" in the financial analysis circles. So for example if the organization has $10 million in debt and $4 million in equity, then the leverage is two point five to one or 2.5:1 – meaning that to every dollar in equity, there is a debt factor of 2.5 . This is considered moderate leverage. High leverage, especially in non-profits is considered as anything north of say 6 or 7 to 1. The higher the leverage the greater the interest cost and the lesser the revenue retention to finance other ministry activities.

While debt is inevitable in today's culture, freedom from debt or certainly debt minimization is utopia and I believe the "Divine" will of God.

Understanding the Income Statement

The genesis of understanding the "income statement" is revenue or intake. I will also take this moment to insert another "Clarkeism": *"It is not how much you take in, it is how much you save."*

As a young man growing up in New York City, working at age 19 while attending university at night, I learned a very valuable lesson on earnings and savings. I worked in a factory with another young man named Caio. We made the same paltry sum of $105 per week but

I was often borrowing from Caio by late in the week and he always seemed to have enough to lend for a small "fee". What did I learn? Caio never spent everything he took in while I spent more than I took in to my detriment but to the benefit of Caio.

The same is true for ministries. I have seen ministries take in staggering amounts in multiple millions and live from Sunday to Sunday while ministries take in a few hundred thousand dollars annually, yet have more in the bank and less stress than the mega organizations. If increased revenue does not lead to greater net asset retention, it means that there are some structural problems within the organization's financial infrastructure.

What I often find out is that Pastors are normally great visionaries but most of us are poor stewards of finances. That is why every organization needs a good chief financial officer ("CFO") with proper qualifications to provide balance and perspective and sometimes even provide a dissenting voice within the organization when it comes to budgetary and financial disbursement issues.

In the introduction I talked about fixed and variable expenses and these two categories of expenses and the management of the latter is central to good revenue retention. Fixed expenses are those expenses that are constant despite what revenue is. For example, the mortgage payment on the ministry building is a constant monthly number.

For presentation purposes I will list some fixed expenses. This list is not all inclusive but should include the major categories of fixed expenses.

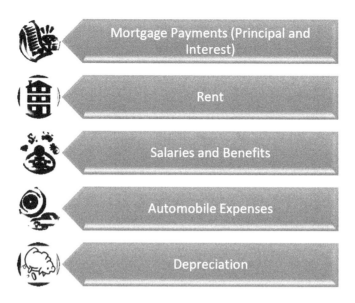

Variable expenses are usually discretionary and can increase and/or decrease along with revenue trajectory. Some variables might include such items as honorariums or outreach and benevolence activities. Some of the most common categories of variable expenses inherent to ministry activities are as follows:

Once all the expenses, both fixed and variable, are deducted from revenue, we then arrive at the revenue retention which in non-profits are referred to as "Net Increase in Assets (or Decrease)". Because the organization is not-for-profit then there is no profit or loss in the true sense of the term and therefore no profit distribution to owners in the form of dividends, etc. Likewise, there are no taxes due as there are no profits to report.

In understanding what cash has been retained from revenue intake and in order to determine the ministry's ability to pay debt service obligations, we must look at cash versus "non-cash" expenses. For example, a ministry might have a net decrease in assets from its operations but have a positive "cash flow". Cash flow in the simplest terms is calculated as follows:

Net Increase / Decrease in Assets

Add:

➢ Depreciation

➢ Amortization

➢ Any other non-cash activity (Does not require a cash outlay)

In the example presented herein, XYZ Church, Inc., we see the following cash flow metrics (Statement of Activities) for the fiscal year 2010-2012 in whole dollars:

Statements of Activities	12 mos 12/31/2012		12 mos 12/31/2011	%	12 mos 12/31/2010	%
Revenue, Support and Gains						
Tithes and offerings	16,861,735		19,785,116		26,024,770	
Sales	444,527		486,374		1,122,220	
Fees	472,858		582,277		911,792	
Tuition						
Rental Income						
Other Income						
Interest and Dividend Income						
Unrealized loss on investments						
Restrictions satisfied by payments						
Total Revenue, Support and Gains	**$17,779,120**	100.0%	**$20,853,767**	100.0%	**$28,058,782**	100.0%
Expenses						
Bank and Finance Charges						
Books, Subscriptions and Curriculum	1,317,732	7.4%	1,850,088	8.9%	3,579,350	12.8%
Childcare		0.0%		0.0%		0.0%
Depreciation	4,764,996	26.8%	4,882,927	23.4%	4,980,413	17.7%
Equipment, Technology and Communications	599,394	3.4%	924,931	4.4%	2,361,472	8.4%
Events, Classes and activities	1,150,028	6.5%	1,509,848	7.2%	2,020,412	7.2%
Fundraising Cost	193,676	1.1%	217,074	1.0%	258,219	0.9%
General expenses		0.0%		0.0%		0.0%
Hospitality. Gifts and Awards		0.0%		0.0%		0.0%
Interest expenses	3,439,481	19.3%	3,264,362	15.7%	3,351,922	11.9%
Kingdom builders		0.0%		0.0%		0.0%
Outreach and Donations	594,265	3.3%	1,326,712	6.4%	5,323,218	19.0%
Performers, Speakers, and Professional		0.0%		0.0%		0.0%
Personnel	2,283,956	12.8%	3,076,738	14.8%	3,589,702	12.8%
Printing, Promotion, Copying and Postage		0.0%		0.0%		0.0%
Rent Expense		0.0%		0.0%		0.0%
Repairs and Maintenance		0.0%		0.0%		0.0%
Retail cost of goods sold		0.0%		0.0%		0.0%
Sub-let expense		0.0%		0.0%		0.0%
Supplies		0.0%		0.0%		0.0%
Taxes, Insurance and Facility costs		0.0%		0.0%		0.0%
Training and Education	6,107,255	34.4%	6,954,533	33.3%	8,018,641	28.6%
Transportation		0.0%		0.0%		0.0%
Total Expenses	**$20,450,783**	115.0%	**$24,007,213**	115.1%	**$33,483,349**	119.3%
Other Revenue and Expenses						
Rental Activities	($1,169,430)		($1,213,154)	-5.8%	$554,092	2.0%
Interest, Divdends,Capital Gains	$51,032		$17,060	0.1%	$60,615	0.2%
Othr Business loss	($140,860)		($247,938)	-1.2%	($407,653)	-1.5%
Unrealized Gain	$3,922		$4,422	0.0%	$2,945	0.0%
Gain on retirement of assets	$3,840		$332,390	1.6%	$294,090	1.0%
Total Other Revenue & Expenses	**($1,251,496)**		**($1,107,220)**	-5.3%	**$504,089**	1.8%
Decrease in Net Assets	(3,923,159)		(4,260,666)		(4,920,478)	
Loss of Disposal of Assets						
Total Decrease in Net Assets	(3,923,159)		(4,260,666)		(4,920,478)	
Add Back: Depreciation	4,764,996		4,882,927		4,980,413	
Amortization						
Net Cash Generated	**$841,837**		**$622,261**		**$59,935**	

The following graph summarizes the net cash flow generated by the organization. As you can see depicted here, we start off with net decrease (loss) in net assets but after we add back depreciation, which is a non-cash expenditure, we then realize a positive net cash flow.

	2012	2011	2010
Total Increase (Decrease) in net assets	<$3,923,159>	<$4,260,666>	<$4,920,478>
Add Back Depreciation	$4,764,996	$4,882,927	$4,980,413
Net Cash Flow	$841,837	$622,261	$59,935

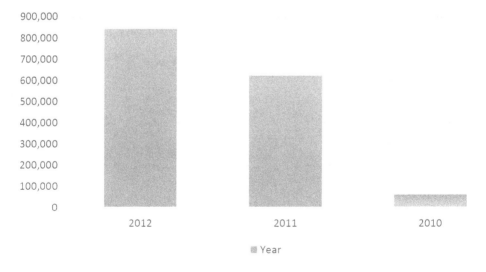

Net Cash Flow Comparison

What does this mean in layman terms? There are a couple of observations and take-a-ways to be made from these figures. These are presented in forms of questions and then explained as follows:

1. *What is the importance of cash flow and how do I view that in relationship to debt service or what is required to pay back the lender?*

   Answer: Cash flow is the net cash generated by the ministry after all expenses have been paid. The expenses must require cash expenditures to be included in this figure. Therefore depreciation for example, is a "non-cash" expenditure and as such is excluded from this calculation. The net cash flow in this case of $841,837 for 2012 is how much the ministry would have available to pay down its debts for example or use for other purposes.

2. *How much can I afford to borrow and at what rate?*

   Answer: The ministry should not borrow more money than the repayment of which can be met by cash flow sufficient to pay principal and interest payments annually. For example, in 2012, in this example, the ministry had $841,837 in cash flow and it also paid the current lender $3,439,481 in interest. So here is the total available in the fiscal year 2012 to:

   1. Pay down the mortgage and
   2. Pay the interest on the mortgage.

   These two usually referred to as P&I were calculated as follows:

   | Cash Flow | $ 841,837 |
   | Interest paid | $3,439,481 |

Available for P&I	$4,281,318

Now most lenders will need to see a Debt Service Coverage Ratio ("DSCR") of say 1.2 times to 1, meaning that the ministry should be able to pay this amount 1.2 times per year before it runs out of money. So in the case of this specific ministry, it could afford a mortgage of $64,000,000 at 1.0X coverage and $53,500,000 at 1.2X coverage.

Those calculations are as follows:

a. Total available for P&I payments annually $4,281,318.
b. This figure equates to $356,778 monthly.
c. Most commercial mortgages of this nature, for example, are amortized over 25 years or 300 months.
d. Let us assume an interest rate of 4.5%. With these 3 givens:
  i. Amount available $4,281,318 annually
  ii. Rate of Interest – 4.5%
  iii. Term of mortgage – 300 N

We then back in how much the mortgage is on a 1.0 times coverage, which in this case is $64,000,000.

On a 1.2 times coverage the amount that could be financed would be calculated as follows:

•	Total cash available	$4,281,318
•	Ratio that is needed	1.2X
•	Annual amount allowed	$3,567,765
•	Monthly amount (/12)	$ 297,138

- Period – 25 Years   300
- Interest rate   4.5%
- Mortgage allowed at 1.2X $53,500,000

I must pause to explain that these are very complex and difficult calculations that need a CFO, CPA or consultancy help to assist the Pastor/President in understanding how this is done.

Using this methodology I suggest that each ministry builds to what it can afford to pay for and not come up with an amount only to find out it cannot afford it. This is a recipe for disaster as warned in Luke 14:28-30.

> "For which of you, intending to build a tower, sitteth not down first, and counteth the cost, whether he have sufficient to finish it? Lest haply, after he hath laid the foundation, and is not able to finish it, all that behold it begin to mock him, Saying, This man began to build, and was not able to finish."
>
> **Luke 14:28-30**

3. *What is "debt coverage ratio" commonly referred to as DSCR?*

   Answer: This means how much cash the ministry has after all cash expenditures, to be able to pay its long term debts such as mortgages.

4. *What is interest only versus principal and interest, and the benefits and downside to both?*

   Answer: Interest only is allowed by some lenders on the initial stage of a mortgage to allow the ministry time to:

   a. Complete a new building.

b. Let its cash flow catch up with the P&I requirements as revenue increases.

This is usually afforded to established ministries with a good cash flow track record. The downside to interest only is that it takes longer to pay off the debt.

Chapter Four

Internal Control Issues

Chapter Four
Internal Control Issues

Choosing a Good Bookkeeping System

Proper internal controls or institutional financial discipline begins with a good record keeping system that generates timely and actionable data. Not only does the ministry needs to know how much was raised but from whom. This allows the ministry to properly evaluate the diversity of its support.

It is also suggested that the system produces monthly financial statements that can be reviewed by the Pastor/President and his/her team. This allows the team to do comparisons.

The Chief Financial Officer ("CFO")

Each institution should have a qualified Chief Financial Officer who, although not necessarily a certified Public Accountant, should have an accounting and finance background. Such a CFO should also have non-profit accounting training and experience. Additionally this CFO must be fairly versed in the regulatory issues unique to non-profits.

Proper Separation of Duties and Transparency

In my opinion, proper separation of duties for the non-profit includes the following:

1. More than one individual handles funds intake. This allows for accountability and transparency.

2. Checks are signed and counter-signed by at least 2 people. While the Pastor/President can be one signor, the co-signor should not be related. This demonstrates some independence and accountability here.

3. Expenditures are approved before commitments to such expenditures are made.

4. Financials should be reviewed monthly by the Pastor/President and the Board.

5. Bank accounts should be reconciled monthly and a listing of all checks written should be available for review by the Pastor/President and Board, if the Board so desires.

6. Annual financial statements should be issued by an external CPA in either a "Review" or "Audited" format.

7. The accounting firm and CPA must be familiar with rules governing non-profits and/or 501(c) 3 organizations.

Chapter Five

The IRS and the 501 (C) 3

Tax Exempt and Government Entities

IRS **EXEMPT ORGANIZATIONS**

Compliance Guide for 501(c)(3) Public Charities

Inside:

Activities that may jeopardize
a charity's exempt status

Federal information returns, tax
returns or notices that must be filed

Recordkeeping—why, what, when

Governance considerations

Changes to be reported to the IRS

Required public disclosures

Resources for public charities

CONTENTS

Compliance
Guide
for 501(c)(3)
Public
Charities

ederal tax law provides tax benefits to nonprofit organizations recognized as exempt from federal income tax under section 501(c)(3) of the Internal Revenue Code (Code). The Code requires that tax-exempt organizations must comply with federal tax law to maintain tax-exempt status and avoid penalties.

In this publication, the IRS addresses activities that could jeopardize a public charity's tax-exempt status. It identifies general compliance requirements on recordkeeping, reporting, and disclosure for exempt organizations (EOs) described in section 501(c)(3) of the Code that are classified as public charities. Content includes references to the statute, Treasury regulations, IRS publications and IRS forms with instructions. Publication 4221-PC is neither comprehensive nor intended to address every situation.

To learn more about compliance rules and procedures that apply to public charities exempt from federal income tax under section 501(c)(3), see IRS Publication 557, *Tax-Exempt Status for Your Organization*, and the *Life Cycle of a Public Charity* on *www.irs.gov/eo*. Stay abreast of new EO information, also on this Web site, by signing up for the *EO Update*, a free newsletter for tax-exempt organizations and practitioners who represent them. For further assistance, consult a tax adviser.

What Activities May Jeopardize a
Public Charity's Tax-Exempt Status?

Once a public charity has completed the application process and has established that it is exempt under section 501(c)(3), the charity's officers, directors, trustees and employees must ensure that the organization maintains its tax-exempt status and meets its ongoing compliance responsibilities.

A 501(c)(3) public charity that does not restrict its participation in certain activities and does not absolutely refrain from others, risks failing the operational test and jeopardizing its tax-exempt status. The following summarizes the limitations on the activities of public charities.

Private Benefit and Inurement

A public charity is prohibited from allowing more than an insubstantial accrual of private benefit to individuals or organizations. This restriction is to ensure that a tax-exempt organization serves a public interest, not a private one. If a private benefit is more than incidental, it could jeopardize the organization's tax-exempt status.

No part of an organization's net earnings may inure to the benefit of an insider. An insider is a person who has a personal or private interest in the activities of the organization such as an officer, director, or a key employee. This means that an organization is prohibited from allowing its income or assets to accrue to insiders. An example of prohibited inurement would include payment of unreasonable compensation to an insider. Any amount of inurement may be grounds for loss of tax-exempt status.

If a public charity provides an economic benefit to any person who is in a position to exercise substantial influence over its affairs (that exceeds the value of any goods or services provided in consideration), the organization has engaged in an excess benefit transaction. A public charity that engages in such a transaction must report it to the IRS. Excise taxes are imposed on any person who engages in an excess benefit transaction with a public charity, and on any organization manager who knowingly approves such a transaction. (See **Reporting Excess Benefit Transactions** on page 12).

A public charity that becomes aware that it may have engaged in an excess benefit transaction should consult a tax advisor and take appropriate action to avoid any potential impact it could have on the organization's continued exempt status. Go to *www.irs.gov/eo* for details about inurement, private benefit, and excess benefit transactions.

Political Campaign Intervention

Public charities are absolutely prohibited from directly or indirectly participating in, or intervening in, any political campaign on behalf of (or in opposition to) a candidate for public office. Contributions to political campaign funds or public statements of position made on behalf of the organization in favor of or in opposition to any candidate for public office clearly violate the prohibition against political campaign activity. Violation of this prohibition may result in revocation of tax-exempt status and/or imposition of certain excise taxes.

Certain activities or expenditures may not be prohibited depending on the facts and circumstances. For example, the conduct of certain voter education activities (including the presentation of public forums and the publication of voter education guides) in a non-partisan manner do not constitute prohibited political campaign activity. Other activities intended to encourage people to participate in the electoral process, such as voter registration and get-out-the-vote drives, would not constitute prohibited political campaign activity if conducted in a non-partisan manner. On the other hand, voter education or registration activities with evidence of bias that would favor

one candidate over another, oppose a candidate in some manner, or have the effect of favoring a candidate or group of candidates, will constitute campaign intervention.

The political campaign activity prohibition is not intended to restrict free expression on political matters by leaders of public charities speaking for themselves as individuals. However, for their organizations to remain tax exempt under section 501(c)(3), organization leaders cannot make partisan comments in official organization publications or at official functions. When speaking in a non-official capacity, these leaders should clearly indicate that their comments are personal, and not intended to represent the views of the organization.

Some section 501(c)(3) organizations take positions on public policy issues, including issues that divide candidates in an election for public office. However, section 501(c)(3) organizations must avoid any issue advocacy that functions as political campaign intervention. Even if a statement does not expressly tell an audience to vote for or against a specific candidate, an organization delivering the statement is at risk of violating the political campaign intervention prohibition if there is any message favoring or opposing a candidate. A statement can identify a candidate not only by stating the candidate's name but also by other means such as showing a picture of the candidate, referring to political party affiliations, or other distinctive features of a candidate's platform or biography. All the facts and circumstances need to be considered to determine if the advocacy is political campaign intervention.

The IRS considers the following factors that tend to show an advocacy communication is political campaign activity:

- whether the statement identifies one or more candidates for a given public office,
- whether the statement expresses approval or disapproval for one or more candidates' positions and/or actions,
- whether the statement is delivered close in time to the election,
- whether the statement makes reference to voting or an election,
- whether the issue addressed in the communication has been raised as an issue distinguishing candidates for a given office,
- whether the communication is part of an ongoing series of communications by the organization on the same issue that are made independent of the timing of any election, and
- whether the timing of the communication and identification of the candidate are related to a non-electoral event such as a scheduled vote on specific legislation by an officeholder who also happens to be a candidate for public office.

A communication is particularly at risk of political campaign intervention when it makes reference to candidates or voting in a specific upcoming election. Nevertheless, the communication must still be considered in context before arriving at any conclusions.

Political candidates may be invited to appear or speak at organization events in their capacity as candidates, or individually (not as a candidate). Candidates may also appear without an invitation at organization events that are open to the public.

When a candidate is invited to speak at a public charity's event as a candidate, factors in determining whether the organization participated or intervened in a political campaign include the following:

- whether the public charity provides an equal opportunity to the political candidates seeking the same office,
- whether the public charity indicates any support of or opposition to the candidate, and
- whether any political fundraising occurs.

When a candidate is invited to speak at a public charity's event in an individual (non-candidate) capacity, factors in determining whether the organization participated or intervened in a political campaign include the following:

- whether the individual is chosen to speak solely for reasons other than candidacy for public office,
- whether the individual speaks in a non-candidate capacity or references his or her candidacy or the election,
- whether the organization maintains a nonpartisan atmosphere on the premises or at the event where the candidate is present, and
- whether the organization clearly indicates the capacity in which the candidate is appearing and does not mention the individual's political candidacy or the upcoming election in the communications announcing the candidate's attendance at the event.

In determining whether candidates are given an equal opportunity to participate, a public charity should consider the nature of the event to which each candidate is invited, in addition to the manner of presentation. For example, a public charity that invites one candidate to speak at its well attended annual banquet, but invites the opposing candidate to speak at a sparsely attended general meeting, will likely be found to have violated the political campaign prohibition, even if the manner of presentation for both speakers is otherwise neutral.

Sometimes a public charity invites several candidates to speak at a public forum. A public forum involving several candidates for public office may qualify as an exempt educational activity. However, if the forum is operated to show a bias for or against any candidate, then the forum would be prohibited campaign activity, as it would be considered intervention or participation in a political campaign. When an organization invites several candidates to speak at a forum, it should consider the following factors:

- whether questions for the candidate are prepared and presented by an independent nonpartisan panel,
- whether the topics discussed by the candidates cover a broad range of issues that the candidates would address if elected to the office sought and are of interest to the public,
- whether each candidate is given an equal opportunity to present his or her views on the issues discussed,
- whether the candidates are asked to agree or disagree with positions, agendas, platforms or statements of the organization, and whether a moderator comments on the questions or otherwise implies approval or disapproval of the candidates.

Read Revenue Ruling 2007-41 at *www.irs.gov/eo* for additional information on the prohibition against political campaign intervention.

When a 501(c)(3) public charity participates in political campaign activity, it jeopardizes both its tax-exempt status and its eligibility to receive tax-deductible contributions. In addition, an excise tax may be imposed in addition to, or instead of, revocation.

Legislative Activities

A public charity is not permitted to engage in substantial legislative activity (commonly referred to as lobbying). An organization will be regarded as attempting to influence legislation if it contacts, or urges the public to contact, members or employees of a legislative body for purposes of proposing, supporting or opposing legislation, or advocates the adoption or rejection of legislation.

If lobbying activities are substantial, a 501(c)(3) organization may fail the operational test and risk losing its tax-exempt status and/or be liable for excise taxes. Substantiality is measured by either the substantial part test or the expenditure test.

The substantial part test determines substantiality on the basis of all the pertinent facts and circumstances in each case. The IRS considers a variety of factors, including the time and expenditures devoted by the organization to the activity, when determining whether the lobbying activity is substantial.

As an alternative, a public charity (other than a church) may elect to use the **expenditure test** by filing Form 5768, *Election/Revocation of Election by an Eligible Section 501(c)(3) Organizations to Make Expenditures to Influence Legislation*. Under the expenditure test, a public charity's lobbying activity will not jeopardize its tax-exempt status provided its expenditures related to lobbying do not normally exceed a set amount specified in section 4911 of the Code. This limit is generally based on the size of the organization and may not exceed $1 million.

Also, under the expenditure test, a public charity that engages in excessive lobbying activity over a four-year period may lose its tax-exempt status, making all of its income for that period subject to tax. Should the organization exceed its lobbying expenditure dollar limit in a particular year, it must pay an excise tax equal to 25 percent of the excess. Read the *Life Cycle of a Public Charity* at www.irs.gov/eo for additional information about the rules against substantial legislative activities.

Public charities that engage in lobbying activities must report lobbying activities on Form 990, Schedule C, *Political Campaign and Lobbying Activities*.

What Federal Information Returns, Tax Returns and Notices Must Be Filed?

While 501(c)(3) public charities are exempt from federal income tax, most of these organizations have information reporting obligations under the Code to ensure that they continue to be recognized as tax-exempt. In addition, they may also be liable for employment taxes, unrelated business income tax, excise taxes, and certain state and local taxes.

Form 990, Return of Organization Exempt From Income Tax, Form 990-EZ, Short Form Return of Organization Exempt From Income Tax and Form 990-N, Electronic Notice (e-Postcard) for Tax-Exempt Organizations Not Required To File Form 990 or 990-EZ

Public charities generally file either a:

- Form 990, *Return of Organization Exempt from Income Tax,*
- Form 990-EZ, *Short Form Return of Organization Exempt from Income Tax,* or
- Form 990-N, *Electronic Notice (e-Postcard) for Tax-Exempt Organizations not Required To File Form 990 or 990-EZ*

The type of Form 990 series return a public charity must file is generally determined by the organization's gross receipts and total assets.

The chart on the next page explains which Form 990 an organization is required to file.

Filing Dates

Forms 990, 990-EZ, and 990-N must be filed by the 15th day of the fifth month after the end of the organization's annual accounting period. The due date for the Forms 990 and 990-EZ may be extended for three months, without showing cause, by filing Form 8868, *Application for Extension of Time To File an Exempt Organization Return,* before the due date. An additional three-month extension may be requested on Form 8868 if the organization shows reasonable cause why the return cannot be filed by the extended due date.

An organization cannot request an extension for filing the Form 990-N; however, there is no penalty for filing it late.

See **Filing Penalties and Revocation of Tax-Exempt Status** on page 13.

Gross Receipts Thresholds	Form to File
Gross receipts normally ≤ **$50,000**	990-N
Gross receipts > **$50,000** and < **$200,000**, and Total assets < **$500,000**	990-EZ or 990
Gross receipts ≥ **$200,000**, or Total assets ≥ **$500,000**	990

Filing Exceptions

Public charities that are not required to file Forms 990 or 990-EZ include:

- churches and certain church-affiliated organizations,
- certain organizations affiliated with governmental units,
- subordinate organizations included in a group return filed by the parent organization, and
- organizations whose annual gross receipts are normally $50,000 or less (see **Form 990-N**, *Electronic Notice (e-Postcard) for Tax-Exempt Organizations not Required To File Form 990 or 990-EZ* on page 12).

If a public charity is excepted from filing a Form 990 or Form 990-EZ because annual gross receipts are normally $50,000 or less, and it elects to file the Form 990 or Form 990-EZ, it must complete the entire return; otherwise, it must file the e-Postcard, Form 990-N, electronically. An organization that only completes those items of information on the Form 990 or Form 990-EZ that are required to be provided on an electronic Form 990-N will not be deemed to have met its electronic notice requirement. See **Form 990-N**, *Electronic Notice (e-Postcard) for Tax-Exempt Organizations Not Required To File Form 990 or 990-EZ* on page 12.

Special Requirements for Supporting Organizations and Donor Advised Funds

Public charities that are supporting organizations described in section 509(a)(3) are generally required to file Form 990 or Form 990-EZ even if their gross receipts are normally $50,000 or less. Supporting organizations of religious organizations need not file Form 990 or Form 990-EZ if their gross receipts are normally $5,000 or less. Such organizations will, however, be required to file the Form 990-N.

Supporting organizations will be required to indicate whether they are a Type 1, Type 2, a Type 3-Functionally Integrated or Type 3-Other supporting organization, identify their supported organizations, and annually certify that they are not controlled by a disqualified person. See the instructions for Schedule A (Form 990 or Form 990-EZ), *Public Charity Status and Public Support* and Notice 2006-109 to determine an organization's appropriate supporting organization type for information return purposes. Learn about new requirements applicable to supporting organizations on the IRS Nonprofits and Charities Web site at *www.irs.gov/eo*.

Sponsoring organizations of donor advised funds (defined as organizations that maintain one or more donor advised funds), and organizations that have controlled entities are required to file Form 990 rather than Form 990-EZ or 990-N.

Form 990 and Form 990-EZ

Form 990 consists of a core form and schedules. Each organization that files the form must complete the entire core form. The core Form 990 includes a Summary Page that provides a "snapshot" of the organization's key financial and operating information for the current and prior year.

All Form 990 filers will provide information about their program service accomplishments, compensation of certain officers, directors and key employees as well as information about governance practices and procedures and financial information.

Each organization that files Form 990 must complete Part IV of Form 990, *Checklist of Required Schedules*, to determine which schedules it must complete based on its activities. See the instructions for Form 990-EZ for information about which schedules 990-EZ filers must complete.

Schedule A, Public Charity Status and Public Support, and Schedule B, Schedule of Contributors

Public charities that file Form 990 or Form 990-EZ must file Schedule A of that return. Schedule A is used to report information about the organization's public charity status and public support.

A new organization will be classified as a public charity, and not a private foundation, for its first five years if it can show that it can reasonably be expected to be publicly supported. If the organization can make this showing, it will be a public charity for its first five years regardless of the public support it actually receives.

The IRS will monitor a new organization's public charity status after the first five years of existence based on the public support information reported annually by the organization on Schedule A of Form 990 based on a five year computation period that consists of the current year and the four years immediately preceding the current year.

Beginning with the organization's sixth year and for all succeeding years, if an organization meets the public support test on Schedule A, the organization will remain a public charity for that current year and the next year.

If a publicly supported charity fails the public support test for two consecutive years, it will be reclassified as a private foundation.

An organization that received an advance ruling determining it a publicly supported organization on or after June 9, 2008, will automatically be classified as a publicly supported organization and need not file Form 8734 at the end of the advance ruling period.

See Publication 4220, *Applying for 501(c)(3) Tax-Exempt Status*, for details on the distinctions between public charities and private foundations. Also go to *www.irs.gov/eo* for additional information on the elimination of the advance ruling process.

Most public charities that received contributions of $5,000 or more from any one contributor must file Schedule B,

Schedule of Contributors. See Part IV, line 2 of Form 990 and the instructions to Schedule B (Form 990, 990-EZ) for complete instructions.

Also see *www.irs.gov/eo* for additional information about other schedules that a public charity may be required to complete based on the nature of its activities.

Reporting Excess Benefit Transactions

If a public charity believes it provided an excess benefit to a person who is in a position to exercise substantial influence over the organization's affairs, it must report the transaction on Form 990 or Form 990-EZ. Excess benefit transactions are governed by section 4958 of the Code. See Appendix G of the Form 990 Instructions for a discussion of section 4958, and Schedule L, Part I, regarding reporting of excess benefit transactions.

Form 990-N, *Electronic Notice (e-Postcard)* for Tax-Exempt Organizations Not Required to File Form 990 or 990-EZ

Any public charity that is not required to file Form 990 or 990-EZ because its annual gross receipts are normally $25,000 or less must instead file Form 990-N, *Electronic Notice (e-Postcard) for Tax-Exempt Organizations Not Required to File Form 990 or Form 990-EZ.* Only churches, their integrated auxiliaries, and conventions or associations of churches, and subordinate organizations included in a group return filed by a parent organization are excused from filing Form 990-N.

The Form 990-N is due by the 15th day of the fifth month after the close of your tax period. For example, if your organization's tax period ends on December 31, 2013, the Form 990-N is due May 15, 2014. The e-Postcard cannot be filed until the organization's tax year ends.

You can access the e-Postcard filing system through the IRS Charities and Nonprofits Web site, *www.irs.gov/eo* or by going directly to the filing system Web site at *http://epostcard. form990.org.*

The form must be completed and filed electronically. There is no paper form.

An organization is required to provide the following information on Form 990-N:

- the organization's legal name,
- any other names the organization uses,
- the organization's mailing address,
- the organization's Web site address (if applicable),
- the organization's employer identification number (EIN), also known as a taxpayer identification number (TIN),
- name and address of a principal officer of the organization,
- the organization's annual tax period,
- confirmation that the organization's annual gross receipts are still normally $50,000 or less, and
- if applicable, a statement that the organization has terminated or is terminating (going out of business).

Read **Filing Penalties and Revocation of Tax-Exempt Status** below on the consequences for failure to file this annual electronic notice and *www.irs.gov/eo* for information about the Form 990-N.

FILING PENALTIES AND REVOCATION OF TAX-EXEMPT STATUS

If a Form 990 or Form 990-EZ is not filed, the IRS may assess penalties on the organization of $20 per day until it is filed. This penalty also applies when the filer fails to include required information or to show correct information. The penalty for failure to file a return or a complete return may not exceed the lesser of $10,000 or 5 percent of the organization's gross receipts. For an organization that has gross receipts of over $1 million for the year, the penalty is $100 a day up to a maximum of $50,000. The IRS may impose penalties on organization managers who do not comply with a written demand that the information be filed.

Section 6033(j) of the Code provides that failure to file Form 990, Form 990-EZ, or Form 990-N for 3 consecutive years results in revocation of tax-exempt status as of the filing due date for the third return. An organization whose exemption is revoked under this section must apply for reinstatement by filing a Form 1023 and paying a user fee, whether or not the organization was originally required to file for exemption. Reinstatement of exemption may be retroactive if the organization shows that the failure to file was for reasonable cause. Information with respect to the implementation of Section 6033(i) is available at *www.irs.gov/eo*.

Public charities with $10 million or more in total assets and that also file at least 250 returns in a calendar year (including income, excise, employment tax, and information returns such as Forms W-2 and 1099) are required to electronically file Form 990. Other public charities are given a choice to file Form 990 electronically. Click on the "IRS *e-file*" logo on the IRS Web site to get the facts on e-filing.

Form 990-T, *Exempt Organization Business Income Tax Return*

A public charity must file a Form 990-T, *Exempt Organization Business Income Tax Return*, if it has $1,000 or more of gross income from an unrelated trade or business during the year. Net income from income-producing activities is taxable if the activities:

- constitute a trade or business,
- are regularly carried on, and
- are not substantially related to the organization's exempt purpose.

Examples of unrelated business income may include income from advertising in publications, income from gaming (except for income from traditional bingo under certain circumstances), and income from the sale of merchandise unrelated to the organization's exempt purpose. Whether an income-producing activity is an unrelated trade or business activity depends on all the facts and circumstances. For more information, see IRS Publication 598, *Tax on Unrelated Business Income of Exempt Organizations*.

The public charity must pay quarterly estimated tax on unrelated business income if it expects its tax for the year to be $500 or more. Form 990-W, *Estimated Tax on Unrelated Business Taxable Income for Tax-Exempt Organizations*, is a worksheet to determine the amount of estimated tax payments required.

Exceptions and Special Rules

Income from certain trade or business activities is excepted from the definition of unrelated business income. Earnings from these sources are not subject to the unrelated business income tax. Exceptions generally include business income from:

An organization may be subject to interest and penalty charges if it files a late return, fails to pay tax when due, or fails to pay estimated tax, if required, even if it did not expect its tax for the year to be $500 or more.

- activities, including fundraisers, that are conducted by volunteer workers, or where donated merchandise is sold;
- activities conducted by a charitable organization or by a governmental college or university for the convenience of members, students, patients or employees;
- qualified conventions and trade shows;
- qualified sponsorship activities; and
- qualified bingo activities.

Income from investments and other "passive" activities is usually excluded from the calculation of unrelated business taxable income. Examples of this type of income include earnings from routine investments such as certificates of deposit, savings accounts, or stock dividends, royalties, certain rents from real property, and certain gains or losses from the sale of property.

Special rules apply to income derived from real estate or other investments purchased with borrowed funds. Such income is called "debt-financed" income. Unrelated debt-financed income generally is subject to the unrelated business income tax.

To learn about unrelated business income, get Publication 598, *Tax on Unrelated Business Income of Exempt Organizations*, Form 990-T instructions, and Form 990-W instructions at *www.irs.gov*.

Employment Tax Returns

Like other employers, all public charities that pay wages to employees must withhold, deposit, and pay employment tax, including federal income tax withholding and Social Security and Medicare (FICA) taxes. A public charity must withhold federal income tax from employee wages and pay FICA on each employee paid $100 or more in wages during a calendar year.

To know how much income tax to withhold, a public charity should have a Form W-4, *Employee's Withholding Allowance Certificate*, on file for each employee. Employment taxes are reported on Form 941, *Employer's Quarterly Federal Tax Return*.

If a small employer (one who has withheld employment taxes of $1,000 or less during the year) has been instructed by IRS to file Form 944, *Employer's Annual Federal Tax Return* instead of Form 941, the employer must do so. The employer must file Form 944 even if there is no tax due or if the taxes exceed $1,000 unless IRS tells it to file Form 941 (or it is filing a final return). See the instructions to Form 944 for information on how to have the filing requirement changed from Form 944 to Form 941.

Any person that fails to withhold and pay employment tax may be subject to penalties. Public charities do not pay federal unemployment (FUTA) tax.

Public charities do not generally have to withhold or pay employment tax on payments to independent contractors, but they may have information reporting requirements. If a charity incorrectly classifies an employee as an independent contractor, it may be held liable for employment taxes for that worker.

The requirements for withholding, depositing, reporting and paying employment taxes are explained in Publication 15, *Circular E, Employer's Tax Guide*. For help in determining if workers are employees or independent contractors, see Publication 15-A, *Employer's Supplemental Tax Guide*. Publication 557, *Tax Exempt Status for Your Organization*, covers the employment tax responsibilities of public charities. These IRS publications can be downloaded at *www.irs.gov*.

Employment Taxes and Churches

Although churches are excepted from filing Form 990, they do have employment tax responsibilities. Employees of churches or church-controlled organizations are subject to income tax withholding, but may be exempt from FICA taxes. Like other 501(c)(3) organizations, churches are not required to pay federal unemployment tax (FUTA). In addition, although ministers generally are common law employees, they are not treated as employees for employment tax purposes. These special employment tax rules for members of the clergy and religious workers are explained in Publication 517, *Social Security and Other Information for Members of the Clergy and Religious Workers*. Churches also should consult Publications 15 and 15-A and Publication 1828, *Tax Guide for Churches and Religious Organizations*.

Why Keep Records?

In general, a public charity must maintain books and records to show that it complies with tax rules. The charity must be able to document the sources of receipts and expenditures reported on Form 990, *Return of Organization Exempt From Income Tax* or Form 990-EZ, *Short Form Return of Organization Exempt From Income Tax*, and Form 990-T, *Exempt Organization Business Income Tax Return*. (See **Prepare Annual Information and Tax Returns** on page 19.)

If an organization does not keep required records, it may not be able to show that it qualifies for tax-exempt status or should be classified as a public charity. Thus, the organization may lose its tax-exempt status or be classified as a private foundation rather than a public charity. In addition, a public charity may be unable to complete its returns accurately and, hence, may be subject to penalties described under **Filing Penalties and Revocation of Tax-Exempt Status** on page 13. When good recordkeeping systems are in place, a public charity can evaluate the success of its programs, monitor its budget, and prepare its financial statements and returns.

Evaluate Charitable Programs

A charity can use records to evaluate the success of its charitable program and determine whether the organization is achieving desired results. Good records can also help a charity identify problem areas and determine what changes it may need to make to improve performance.

Monitor Budgetary Results

Without proper financial records, it is difficult for a charity to assess whether it has been successful in adhering to budgetary guidelines. The ability to monitor income and expenses and ensure that the organization is operating within its budget is crucial to successful stewardship of a public charity.

Prepare Financial Statements

It is important to maintain sufficient financial information in order to prepare accurate and timely annual financial statements. A charity may need these statements when it is working with banks, creditors, contributors, and funding organizations. Some states require charities to make audited financial statements publicly available.

Prepare Annual Information and Tax Returns

Records must support income, expenses, and credits reported on Form 990 series and other tax returns. Generally, these are the same records used to monitor programs and prepare financial statements. Books and records of public charities must be available for inspection by the IRS. If the IRS examines a public charity's returns, the organization must have records to explain items reported. Having a complete set of records will speed up the examination.

Identify Sources of Receipts

Public charities may receive money or property from many sources. With thorough recordkeeping, a charity can identify the sources of receipts. Organizations need this information to separate program from non-program receipts, taxable from non-taxable income, and to complete Schedule A, as well as other schedules of the Form 990 the organization may be required to complete, noted in **What Federal Information Returns, Tax Returns, and Notices Must be Filed?** on page 8. An organization should maintain a list of its donors and grantors and the amount of cash contributions or grants (or a description of the noncash contributions) received from each.

Substantiate Revenues, Expenses and Deductions for Unrelated Business Income Tax (UBIT) Purposes

An organization needs to keep records of revenues derived from, and expenses attributable to, an unrelated trade or business so that it can properly prepare Form 990-T and calculate its unrelated business taxable income.

Comply with Grant-Making Procedures (Grants to Individuals)

A public charity that makes grants to individuals must keep adequate records and case histories to demonstrate that such grants serve its charitable purposes. Case histories on grants to individuals should show names, addresses, purposes of grants, manner of selection, and relationship (if any) that the recipient has with any members, officers, trustees, or donors of the organization. For more information about appropriate records required to report on grants made within the United States, see Schedule I of Form 990 and instructions. See also Schedule F of Form 990 for information about records required to report on foreign grants.

Private schools must keep records that show that they have
complied with requirements relating to racial non-discrimination,
including annual publication of a racially nondiscriminatory
policy through newspaper or broadcast media to the general
community served. For more information, see Schedule E of
Form 990.

What Records Should be Kept?

Except in a few cases, the law does not require a special
kind of record. A public charity can choose any recordkeeping
system, suited to its activities, that clearly shows the organization's income and expenses. The types of activities a public
charity conducts determines the type of records that should be
kept for federal tax purposes. A public charity should set up
a recordkeeping system using an accounting method that is
appropriate for proper monitoring and reporting of its financial
activities for the tax year. If a public charity has more than
one program, it should ensure that the records appropriately
identify the income and expense items that are attributable to
each program.

A recordkeeping system should generally include a summary
of transactions. This summary is ordinarily written in the public
charity's books (for example, accounting journals and ledgers).
The books must show gross receipts, purchases, expenses
(other than purchases), employment taxes, and assets. For
most small organizations, the checkbook might be the main
source for entries in the books while larger organizations would
need more sophisticated ledgers and records. A public charity
must keep documentation that supports entries in the books.

RECORDS MANAGEMENT

GROSS RECEIPTS

Gross receipts are the amounts received from all sources, including contributions. A public charity should keep supporting documents that show the amounts and sources of its gross receipts. Documents that show gross receipts include: donor correspondence, pledge documents, cash register tapes, bank deposit slips, receipt books, invoices, credit card charge slips, and Forms 1099-MISC, *Miscellaneous Income*.

PURCHASES, INCLUDING ACCOUNTING FOR INVENTORY

Purchases are items bought, including any items resold to customers. If an organization produces items, it must account for any items resold to customers. Thus, for example, the organization must account for the cost of all raw materials or parts purchased for manufacture into finished products. Supporting documents should show the amount paid, and that the amount was for purchases. Documents for purchases include: canceled checks, cash register tape receipts, credit card sales slips, and invoices. These records will help a public charity determine the value of its inventory at the end of the year. See Publication 538, *Accounting Periods and Methods*, for general information on methods for valuing inventory.

EXPENSES

Expenses are the costs a public charity incurs (other than purchases) to carry on its program. Supporting documents should show the amount paid and the purpose of the expense. Documents for expenses include: canceled checks, cash register tapes, contracts, account statements, credit card sales slips, invoices, and petty-cash slips for small cash payments.

EMPLOYMENT TAXES

Organizations that have employees must keep records of compensation and specific employment tax records. See Publication 15, *Circular E, Employer's Tax Guide*, for details.

Assets are the property, such as investments, buildings, and furniture that an organization owns and uses in its activities. Liabilities reflect the pecuniary obligations of the organization. A public charity must keep records to verify certain information about its assets and liabilities. Records should show:

- when and how the asset was acquired
- whether any debt was used to acquire the asset
- documents that support mortgages, notes, loans or other forms of debt
- purchase price
- cost of any improvements
- deductions taken for depreciation, if any
- deductions taken for casualty losses, if any, such as losses resulting from fires or storms
- how the asset was used
- when and how the asset was disposed of
- selling price
- expenses of sale

Documents that may show the above information include: purchase and sales invoices, real estate closing statements, canceled checks, and financing documents. If a public charity does not have canceled checks, it may be able to show payment with certain financial account statements prepared by financial institutions. These include account statements prepared for the financial institution by a third party. All information, including account statements, must be highly legible. The following defines acceptable account statements.

IF payment is by:	**THEN** statement must show:
check	check number, amount, payee's name, and date the check amount was posted to the account by the financial institution
electronic funds transfer	amount transferred, payee's name, and date the transfer was posted to the account by the financial institution
credit card	amount charged, payee's name, and transaction date

Accounting Periods and Methods

A public charity must keep its books and records based on an annual accounting period called a tax year in order to comply with annual reporting requirements.

Accounting Periods — A tax year is usually 12 consecutive months. There are two kinds of tax years.

calendar tax year – This is a period of 12 consecutive months beginning January 1 and ending December 31.

fiscal tax year – This is a period of 12 consecutive months ending on the last day of any month except December.

Accounting Method — An accounting method is a set of rules used to determine when and how income and expenses are reported. A public charity chooses an accounting method when it files its first annual return. There are two basic accounting methods:

cash method – Under the cash method, a public charity reports income in the tax year received. It usually deducts expenses in the year paid.

accrual method – Under an accrual method, a public charity generally records income in the tax year earned, (i.e., in the tax year in which a pledge is received, even though it may receive payment in a later year.) It records expenses in the tax year incurred, whether or not it pays the expenses that year.

For more information about accounting periods and methods, see Publication 538, *Accounting Periods and Methods*, and the instructions to Form 990 and Form 990-EZ.

Supporting Documents

Organization transactions such as contributions, purchases, sales, and payroll will generate supporting documents. These documents — grant applications and awards, sales slips, paid bills, invoices, receipts, deposit slips, and canceled checks — contain information to be recorded in accounting records. It is important to keep these documents because they support the entries in books and the entries on tax and information returns. Public charities should keep supporting documents organized by year and type of receipt or expense. Also, keep records in a safe place.

How Long Should Records be Kept?

Public charities must keep records for federal tax purposes for as long as they may be needed to document evidence of compliance with provisions of the Code. Generally, this means the organization must keep records that support an item of income or deduction on a return until the statute of limitations for that return runs. The statute of limitations has run when the organization can no longer amend its return and the IRS can no longer assess additional tax. Generally, the statute of limitations runs three years after the date the return is due or filed, whichever is later. An organization may be required to retain records longer for other legal purposes, including state or local tax purposes.

Record Retention Periods

Record retention periods vary depending on the types of records and returns.

Permanent Records — Some records should be kept permanently. These include the application for recognition of tax-exempt status, the determination letter recognizing tax-exempt status, and organizing documents, such as articles of incorporation and by-laws, with amendments, as well as board minutes.

Employment Tax Records – If an organization has employees, it must keep employment tax records for at least four years after the date the tax becomes due or is paid, whichever is later.

Records for Non-Tax Purposes – When records are no longer needed for tax purposes, an organization should keep them until they are no longer needed for non-tax purposes. For example, a grantor, insurance company, creditor, or state agency may require that records be kept longer than the IRS requires.

What Governance Procedures and Practices Should an Organization Consider Adopting or Have In Place?

While federal law does not mandate any particular management structures, operational policies or administrative practices, it is important that public charities be thoughtful about the governance practices that are most appropriate for that charity in assuring sound operations and compliance with the tax law. While you may not be required to have one policy or another, the IRS is authorized by section 6033 to ask for information we consider to be relevant to tax administration, including governance.

Mission Statement and Organizational Documents

The IRS encourages every charity to adopt, establish and regularly review a mission statement to explain the organization's purposes and guide its work. Significant changes in your organizational documents should be reported to the IRS, as noted below.

Governing Body

An active and engaged board is important to the success of a public charity and compliance with the tax law. A governing board should be composed of persons who are informed and active in overseeing a charity's operations and finances. To guard against insider transactions that could result in misuse of charitable assets, the governing board should include independent members and should not be dominated by employees or others who are not independent because of business or family relationships.

Although the Internal Revenue Code does not require charities to have particular governance and management polices, the IRS does encourage boards of charities to consider whether the implementation of policies relating to executive compensation, conflicts of interest, investments, fundraising, documentation of governance decisions, document retention, and whistleblower claims may be necessary and appropriate.

Further, if a public charity has chapters or affiliates, it is encouraged to have procedures or policies in place to ensure consistency in operations.

Board members are encouraged to regularly review the organization's financial statements and information returns, and consider whether an independent auditor is appropriate.

Public charities are encouraged to adopt and monitor procedures to ensure that information about their mission, activities, finance and governance is made publicly available. Go to *www.irs.gov/eo* for more information about governance.

How Should Changes be Reported to the IRS?

Reporting Changes on the Annual Information Return

A public charity that is required to file Form 990 or Form 990-EZ must report name, address, structural and operational changes on its annual information return. Regardless of whether a public charity files an annual information return, it may also report these changes to the EO Determinations Office at the mailing address set out in **How to Get IRS Assistance and Information** on page 33; however, such reporting does not relieve the organization from reporting the changes on its annual information return. For information about informing the IRS of a termination or merger see Pub 4779, *Facts About Terminating or Merging Your Exempt Organization*.

Tip: Attach copies of any signed or state certified articles of incorporation or association, constitution or trust instrument or other organizing document, or the bylaws or other governing document showing changes to your return. If signed or state certified copies of a governing document are not available, an authorized officer may certify that the governing document provided is a complete and accurate copy of the original document.

Determination Letters and Private Letter Ruling Requests

A public charity may request a copy of a lost exemption letter or an updated exemption letter that reflects a name or address change from the EO Determinations office. A public charity that has had a change in its public charity or private foundation status should request a new determination letter from the EO Determinations office as well. See **How to Get IRS Assistance and Information** on page 33 for the appropriate address for the EO Determinations office.

An organization may request a *determination letter* regarding the effect of certain changes on its tax exempt status or public charity status. For example, as noted above, a determination letter will be issued to classify or reclassify an organization as a public charity or a private foundation. A public charity may also request a determination letter to approve the treatment of a contribution as an unusual grant, or to determine whether an organization is exempt from filing annual information returns in certain situations. However, the IRS will not make any determination regarding any completed transaction.

If a public charity is unsure about whether a proposed change in its purposes or activities is consistent with its status as an exempt organization or as a public charity, it may want to request a *private letter ruling.*

The IRS issues *private letter rulings* on *proposed* transactions and on completed transactions — if the request is submitted before the return is filed for the year in which the transaction was completed. The IRS generally does not issue rulings to public charities on any other completed transactions. The IRS will issue letter rulings to public charities on matters involving a public charity's exempt status, its public charity status, as well as other matters including issues under sections 501 through 514, 4911, 4912, 4955, 4958, 6033, 6104, and 6115.

Consult *www.irs.gov/eo* for the appropriate procedures for preparing and submitting a request for a determination letter, private letter ruling, replacement exemption letter or a letter reflecting a new name and address. For general information about reporting changes, you may contact EO customer service at (877)829-5500.

What Disclosures are Required?

There are a number of disclosure requirements for public charities. Detailed information on federal tax law disclosure requirements for 501(c)(3) tax-exempt organizations can be found in Publication 557, *Tax Exempt Status for Your Organization*, on the IRS Charities and Nonprofits Web site at *www.irs.gov/eo*.

Public Inspection of Annual Returns and Exemption Applications

A public charity must make the following documents available for public inspection and copying upon request and without charge (except for a reasonable charge for copying). The IRS also makes these documents available for public inspection and copying. A public charity may place reasonable restrictions on the time, place, and manner of in person inspection and copying, and may charge a reasonable fee for providing copies. It can charge no more for the copies than the per page rate the IRS charges for providing copies. See *www.irs.gov/foia/index.html* for current IRS copying fees. Although the IRS charges no fee for the first 100 pages, the organization can charge a fee for all copies. The organization can also charge the actual postage costs it pays to provide copies. A tax-exempt organization does not have to comply with individual requests for copies if it makes the documents widely available. This can be done by posting the documents on a readily accessible Web site.

For details on disclosure rules and procedures for public charities, see *Life Cycle of a Public Charity* and the instructions to Forms 990 and 1023 at *www.irs.gov/eo*.

Because certain forms, by law, must be made publicly available by the IRS and the filer, do not include any personal identifying information, such as social security numbers not required by the IRS, on these forms.

Exemption Application - A public charity must make available for public inspection its exemption application, Form 1023, *Application for Recognition of Exemption Under Section 501(c)(3) of the Internal Revenue Code*, along with each of the following documents:

- all documents submitted with Form 1023;
- all documents the IRS requires the organization to submit in support of its application; and
- the exemption ruling letter issued by the IRS.

Annual Information Return - A public charity must make available for public inspection its annual information return (Form 990 series) with schedules, attachments, and supporting documents filed with the IRS. However, a public charity that files a Form 990 or Form 990-EZ does not have to disclose the names and addresses of contributors listed on Schedule B. All other information, including the amount of contributions, the description of noncash contributions, and any other information provided will be open to public inspection unless it clearly identifies the contributor.

Note: If an organization files a copy of Form 990 or Form 990-EZ, and attachments, with any state, it should not include its Schedule B in the attachments for the state, unless a schedule of contributors is specifically required by the state. States that do not require the information might inadvertently make the schedule available for public inspection along with the rest of the Form 990 or Form 990-EZ.

Certain information may be withheld from public inspection. A return must be made available for a period of three years from the date the return is required to be filed or is actually filed, whichever is later.

Form 990-T - A public charity must make Form 990-T available for the three years beginning on the last day (including extensions) for filing the return. Schedules, attachments and supporting documents filed with Form 990-T that do not relate to unrelated business income tax are not required to be made available. Read Notice 2007-45 and Notice 2008-49 at *www.irs.gov* for interim guidance regarding how the returns are to be made public. See Announcement 2008-21 for procedures the public may use to request a 501(c)(3) organization's Form 990-T from the IRS.

Public Inspection and Disclosure Procedures A public charity may place reasonable restrictions on the time, place, and manner of in-person inspection and copying, and may charge a reasonable fee for providing copies. It can charge no more for the copies than the per page rate the IRS charges for providing copies. A tax-exempt organization does not have to comply with individual requests for copies if it makes the documents widely available. This can be done by posting the documents on a readily accessible Web site. For details on disclosure rules and procedures for 501(c)(3) organizations, see the *Life Cycle of a Public Charity* and the instructions to Forms 990, 990-T and 1023 at *www.irs.gov/eo.*

All publicly-available information may be obtained from the IRS for a fee by using Form 4506-A, *Request for Public Inspection or Copy of Exempt or Political Organization IRS Form.* An organization may obtain a complete copy of its own application by filing Form 4506, *Request for Copy of Tax Return.*

PENALTIES

Penalties apply to responsible persons of a tax-exempt organization who fail to provide the documents as required. A penalty of $20 per day may apply for as long as the failure continues. A $10,000 maximum penalty applies to a failure to provide an information return; no maximum penalty applies to application requests.

Sale of Free Government Information

If a public charity offers to sell, or solicits money for, specific information or a routine service that is available free from the federal government, the organization must make an express statement at the time of solicitation about the free service. An organization that intentionally disregards this requirement is subject to a penalty.

Charitable Contributions— Substantiation and Disclosure

A public charity should be aware of the substantiation and recordkeeping rules imposed on donors who intend to claim a charitable contribution deduction and the disclosure rules imposed on charities that receive certain *quid pro quo* contributions.

Recordkeeping Rules

A donor cannot claim a tax deduction for any cash, check, or other monetary contribution made on or after January 1, 2007, unless the donor maintains a record of the contribution in the form of either a bank record (such as a cancelled check) or a written communication from the charity (such as a receipt or a letter) showing the name of the charity, date, and the amount of the contribution.

Substantiation Rules

A donor cannot claim a tax deduction for any single contribution of $250 or more unless the donor obtains a contemporaneous written acknowledgment of the contribution from the recipient public charity. A public charity may assist the donor by providing a timely written statement including the name of the public charity, date and amount of any cash contribution, and description of any non-cash contributions.

In addition, the acknowledgment should indicate whether any goods or services were provided in return for the contribution. If any goods or services were provided in return for a contribution, the organization should provide a description and good faith estimate of the value of such goods or services.

The public charity may either provide separate acknowledgments for each single contribution of $250 or more or one acknowledgment to substantiate several single contributions of $250 or more. Separate contributions are not aggregated for purposes of measuring the $250 threshold.

Public Inspection and Disclosure Procedures — A public charity may place reasonable restrictions on the time, place, and manner of in-person inspection and copying, and may charge a reasonable fee for providing copies. It can charge no more for the copies than the per page rate the IRS charges for providing copies. A tax-exempt organization does not have to comply with individual requests for copies if it makes the documents widely available. This can be done by posting the documents on a readily accessible Web site. For details on disclosure rules and procedures for 501(c)(3) organizations, see the *Life Cycle of a Public Charity* and the instructions to Forms 990, 990-T and 1023 at *www.irs.gov/eo*.

All publicly-available information may be obtained from the IRS for a fee by using Form 4506-A, *Request for Public Inspection or Copy of Exempt or Political Organization IRS Form*. An organization may obtain a complete copy of its own application by filing Form 4506, *Request for Copy of Tax Return*.

PENALTIES

Penalties apply to responsible persons of a tax-exempt organization who fail to provide the documents as required. A penalty of $20 per day may apply for as long as the failure continues. A $10,000 maximum penalty applies to a failure to provide an information return; no maximum penalty applies to application requests.

Sale of Free Government Information

If a public charity offers to sell, or solicits money for, specific information or a routine service that is available free from the federal government, the organization must make an express statement at the time of solicitation about the free service. An organization that intentionally disregards this requirement is subject to a penalty.

Charitable Contributions— Substantiation and Disclosure

A public charity should be aware of the substantiation and recordkeeping rules imposed on donors who intend to claim a charitable contribution deduction and the disclosure rules imposed on charities that receive certain *quid pro quo* contributions.

Recordkeeping Rules

A donor cannot claim a tax deduction for any cash, check, or other monetary contribution made on or after January 1, 2007, unless the donor maintains a record of the contribution in the form of either a bank record (such as a cancelled check) or a written communication from the charity (such as a receipt or a letter) showing the name of the charity, date, and the amount of the contribution.

Substantiation Rules

A donor cannot claim a tax deduction for any single contribution of $250 or more unless the donor obtains a contemporaneous written acknowledgment of the contribution from the recipient public charity. A public charity may assist the donor by providing a timely written statement including the name of the public charity, date and amount of any cash contribution, and description of any non-cash contributions.

In addition, the acknowledgment should indicate whether any goods or services were provided in return for the contribution. If any goods or services were provided in return for a contribution, the organization should provide a description and good faith estimate of the value of such goods or services.

The public charity may either provide separate acknowledgments for each single contribution of $250 or more or one acknowledgment to substantiate several single contributions of $250 or more. Separate contributions are not aggregated for purposes of measuring the $250 threshold.

There are no IRS forms for the acknowledgment. Letters, postcards, or computer-generated forms with the above information are acceptable. An organization can provide either a paper copy of the acknowledgment or an electronic acknowledgment, such as an e-mail, to the donor.

Disclosure Rules That Apply to Quid Pro Quo Contributions

Contributions are deductible only to the extent that they are gifts and no consideration is received in return. Depending on the circumstances, ticket purchases and similar payments made in conjunction with fundraising events may not qualify as charitable contributions in full. A contribution made by a donor in exchange for goods or services is known as a *quid pro quo* contribution. A donor may only take a charitable contribution deduction to the extent that the contribution exceeds the fair market value of the goods and services the donor receives in return for the contribution.

If a public charity conducts fundraising events such as benefit dinners, shows, and membership drives, where something of value is given to those in attendance, it must provide a written statement informing donors of the fair market value of the specific items or services it provided in exchange for contribu-tions. Token items and services of intangible religious value need not be taken into account. A public charity should pro-vide the written disclosure statement in advance of any event, determine the fair market value of any benefit received, and state this information in fundraising materials such as solicita-tions, tickets, and receipts. The disclosure statement should be made, at the latest, at the time payment is received. Subject to certain exceptions, the disclosure responsibility applies to any fundraising circumstance where each complete payment, including the contribution portion, exceeds $75.

Read Publication 1771, *Charitable Contributions—Substantiation and Disclosure Requirements*, and Publication 526, *Charitable Contributions*, for details on the federal tax law for organiza-tions such as public charities, including churches, that receive tax-deductible charitable contributions and for taxpayers who make contributions.

The IRS offers help that is accessible
online, via mail, by telephone, and
at IRS walk-in offices in many areas
across the country. IRS forms and
publications can be downloaded
from the Internet and ordered
by telephone.

Specialized Assistance for Tax-Exempt Organizations

Get help with questions about applying
for tax-exempt status, annual filing
requirements, and information about
exempt organizations from the IRS
Exempt Organizations (EO) pages
on the IRS website, at www.irs.gov/
Charities-&-Non-Profits.

EO Web site	*www.irs.gov/eo*

Highlights:

- *The Life Cycle of a Public Charity* describes the compliance obligations of charities.

- Subscribe to the *EO Update*, an electronic newsletter with information for tax-exempt organizations and tax practitioners who represent them.

EO Web-based Training	*www.stayexempt.irs.gov*

EO Customer Service	(877) 829-5500

EO Determinations Office Mailing Address

Internal Revenue Service
TE/GE, EO Determinations Office
P.O. Box 2508
Cincinnati, OH 45201

Tax Publications for Exempt Organizations

Get publications via the Internet or by calling the IRS at (800) 829-3676.

Pub 1, *Your Rights as a Taxpayer*

Pub 15, *Circular E, Employer's Tax Guide*

Pub 15-A, *Employer's Supplemental Tax Guide*

Pub 463, *Travel, Entertainment, Gift, and Car Expenses*

Pub 517, *Social Security and Other Information for Members of the Clergy and Religious Workers*

Pub 526, *Charitable Contributions*

Pub 538, *Accounting Periods and Methods*

Pub 557, *Tax-Exempt Status for Your Organization*

Pub 571, *Tax-Sheltered Annuity Plans (403(b) Plans) for Employees of Public Schools and Certain Tax-Exempt Organizations*

Pub 583, *Starting a Business and Keeping Records*

Pub 598, *Tax on Unrelated Business Income of Exempt Organizations*

Pub 1771, *Charitable Contributions — Substantiation and Disclosure Requirements*

Pub 1828, *Tax Guide for Churches and Religious Organizations*

Pub 3079, *Tax-Exempt Organizations and Gaming*

Pub 3833, *Disaster Relief, Providing Assistance Through Charitable Organizations*

Pub 4220, *Applying for 501(c)(3) Tax-Exempt Status*

Pub 4221-NC, *Compliance Guide for Tax-Exempt Organizations (other than 501(c)(3) Public Charities and Private Foundations)*

Pub 4221-PF, *Compliance Guide for 501(c)(3) Private Foundations*

Pub 4302, *A Charity's Guide to Vehicle Donations*

Pub 4303, *A Donor's Guide to Vehicle Donations*

Pub 4630, *Exempt Organizations Products and Services Catalog*

Pub 4779, *Facts about Terminating or Merging Your Exempt Organization*

Forms for Exempt Organizations

Get forms via the Internet or by calling the IRS at (800) 829-3676.

Form 941, *Employer's Quarterly Federal Tax Return*

Form 944, *Employer's Annual Federal Tax Return*

Form 990, *Return of Organization Exempt From Income Tax*

Form 990-EZ, *Short Form Return of Organization Exempt From Income Tax*

Form 990-PF, *Return of Private Foundation or Section 4947(a)(1) Nonexempt Charitable Trust Treated as a Private Foundation*

Form 990-N, *Electronic Notice (e-Postcard) For Tax-Exempt Organizations Not Required To File Form 990 or 990-EZ* (only available electronically)

Form 990-T, *Exempt Organization Business Income Tax Return*

Form 990-W, *Estimated Tax on Unrelated Business Taxable Income for Exempt Organizations*

Form 1023, *Application for Recognition of Exemption Under Section 501(c)(3) of the Internal Revenue Code*

Form 1024, *Application for Recognition of Exemption Under Section 501(a)*

Form 1041, *U.S. Income Tax Return for Estates and Trusts*

Form 4720, *Return of Certain Excise Taxes Under Chapters 41 and 42 of the Internal Revenue Code*

continued next page

Form 5578, *Annual Certification of Racial Non-Discrimination for a Private School Exempt from Federal Income Tax*

Form 5768, *Election/Revocation of Election by an Eligible Section 501(c)(3) Organization to Make Expenditures to Influence Legislation*

Form 8282, *Donee Information Return*

Form 8283, *Noncash Charitable Contributions*

Form 8868, *Application for Extension of Time to File an Exempt Organization Return*

TD F 90-22.1, *Report of Foreign Bank and Financial Accounts*

General IRS Assistance

Get materials on the latest tax laws, assistance with forms and publications, and filing information.

IRS Web site	***www.irs.gov***
Federal tax questions	(800) 829-4933
Employment tax questions	(800) 829-4933
Order IRS forms and publications	(800) 829-3676

Chapter Six
Key Things to Remember

Chapter Six
Key Things To Remember

As I summarize this presentation, I was inspired to put down a few things in a "cheat sheet" format of things that the effective financial management of non-profits dictate. Firstly as shown in Proverbs 24:30-34, proper management of Kingdom resources is hard work and there is no way around it. It requires constant due diligence and tweaking in real-time due to its volatile nature. Let's put it this way: *"If it were that easy everyone would be successful"* ("Clarkeism")

"I went past the field of a sluggard, past the vineyard of someone who has no sense; thorns had come up everywhere, the ground was covered with weeds, and the stone wall was in ruins. I applied my heart to what I observed and learned a lesson from what I saw: A little sleep, a little slumber, a little folding of the hands to rest—and poverty will come on you like a thief and scarcity like an armed man."

Proverbs 24:30-34

As shown in Proverbs 10:4, laziness or intransigence leads to poverty while diligent hands bring wealth. Plan to be successful and always remember that success is where good planning intersects with opportunity.

"Lazy hands make for poverty, but diligent hands bring wealth."

Proverbs 10:4

- ❖ The Pastor/President must have a basic understanding of cash flow, liquidity, budgeting and interpretation of financial metrics to be able to talk intelligently and offer guidance to those they lead.

- ❖ Churches and non-profits are businesses and proper financial management is a key ingredient to their reputations, successes and longevity.

- ❖ To venture into debt obligations before ensuring that one has the means to repay such debt is irresponsible, precipitous and is like a hunter who shoots first and aims after.

- ❖ The non-profit must also secure "seed money" from its members to start up but also equally important, like regular businesses who retain a part of their earnings to boost their equity and ease their debt reliance, the non-profit must always seek to retain a part of its intake.

- ❖ Effectively managing finances begins with proper accounting policies and procedures. Internal controls and disciplines are at the core of good financial management.

- ❖ It is important to know what the current financial condition of the organization is and on a real-time basis.

- ❖ Debt minimization leads to more retention of revenue down to equity eventually because the cost of debt is lessened.

- ❖ The higher the leverage, the greater the interest cost and the lesser the revenue retention to finance other ministry activities. While debt is inevitable in today's culture, freedom from debt or certainly debt minimization is utopia and I believe the "Divine" will of God.

❖ Public charities are absolutely prohibited from directly or indirectly participating in, or intervening in, any political campaign on behalf of (or in opposition to) a candidate for public office.

❖ Public charities generally file either a:

  ○ Form 990, *Return of Organization Exempt from Income Tax*,
  ○ Form 990-EZ, *Short Form Return of Organization Exempt from Income Tax*, or
  ○ Form 990-N, Electronic Notice *(e-Postcard) for Tax-Exempt Organizations not Required to file Form 990 or 990-E.*

❖ Forms 990, 990-EZ, and 990-N must be filed by the 15th day of the fifth month after the end of the organization's annual accounting period.

❖ The IRS will monitor a new organization's public charity status after the first five years of existence based on the public support information reported annually by the organization on Schedule A of Form 990 based on a five year computation period that consists of the current year and the four years immediately preceding the current year.

❖ A public charity must keep its books and records based on an annual accounting period called a tax year in order to comply with annual reporting requirements.

List of "Clarkeisms"

- Too many times the Pastor/President is busy trying to get folks to heaven while the organization's finances are on their way to hell.

- Never spend more than you take in and never spend everything you take in.

- God is an owner, not a renter.

- It is not how much you take in, it is how much you save.

- If it were that easy, everyone would be successful.

- Information without transformation leads to frustration.

References

Chapter 5:

Publication 4221-PC (Rev. 8-2013) Catalog Number 49829R,

Department of the Treasury Internal Revenue Service,

www.irs.gov

Endorsements

....

"This book is amazing, very educational and a great tool for effectively managing finances of churches and non-profits!"

Jose Santodomingo, CPA

"Don Clarke is a highly credible source for providing assistance to churches as it pertains to financial matters. His skills and expertise both in the non-profit and financial arenas bring a much needed support to churches and not-for-profits."

Steve Worthington, Executive Vice President,
Evangelical Christian Credit Union

"In my 30 plus years of law practice, rarely have I encountered a professional such as Dr. Clarke, a man blessed with the special combination of Godly wisdom and practical insight which has consistently translated into success for the ministries and non-profit organizations that have had the benefit of his energy, leadership, guidance and advice."

R. Steven Jones, Esq.,
Jones, Davis & Jackson, PC

"Don's long time experience in the financial industry goes beyond financial literacy. His ability to understand the global financial picture is the trait that sets him apart from others and makes him an invaluable asset to me."

Steve Redlich, Executive Vice President,
Bank United

CPSIA information can be obtained
at www.ICGtesting.com
Printed in the USA
LVHW06s0146210818
587591LV00010B/247/P